GET THE SCOOP

on Animal PUKE!

GET THE SCOOP

on Animal PUKE!

**From Zombie Ants to Vampire Bats,
251 Cool Facts about Vomit,
Regurgitation, & More!**

Dawn Cusick

Imagine
Publishing

to Charles Nurnberg,
whose belief in the power
of books has changed many lives

An Imagine Book
Published by Charlesbridge
85 Main Street
Watertown, MA 02472
(617) 926-0329
www.charlesbridge.com

Library of Congress Cataloging-in-Publication Data is
available upon request.

ISBN: 978-1-62354-045-6

Printed in China. Manufactured in March, 2014.

(hc) 10 9 8 7 6 5 4 3 2 1

Display type and text type set in Geometric Slab and Magelsom.

Jacket and Type Design: Celia Naranjo
Proofreading: Meredith Hale
Beta Testers: Hall Fletcher Elementary School
Produced by EarlyLight Books

For information about custom editions, special sales,
premium and corporate purchases, please contact
Charlesbridge Publishing at specialsales@charlesbridge.com.

CONTENTS

INTRODUCTION   8 & 9

LANGUAGE MATTERS   10 & 11

WHY ANIMALS PUKE   12 & 13

NO PUKERS HERE   14 & 15

PEOPLE PUKE   16 & 17

PUKE DEFENSE   20 & 21

TOXIC PUKE DEFENSE   22 & 23

INDIGESTIBLE PUKE   24-29

BABY PUKERS   30 & 31

PUKE SOUP   32 & 33

PUKE DETECTIVES   34 & 35

CUD PUKERS   36-43

COURTSHIP PUKE   44 & 45

PUKE FEEDERS   46-54

PUKE BUILDERS   55-57

PARASITE PUKE   58 & 59

HOUSEKEEPING PUKE   60-61

ROCK PUKERS   62

PUKING STOMACHS   63

CLEAN IT UP!   64 & 65

WILD & WACKY   66-68

PUKE INTERVIEWS   69-71

LEARN MORE   72 & 73

GLOSSARY   74

RESEARCH & READING   75

INDEXES & ACKNOWLEDGMENTS   76-79

INTRODUCTION

Welcome!

Some things in nature seem very gross when you first hear about them. If you learn why and how something happens, though, nature becomes more fascinating and less disgusting. For example, as you quietly read the words on this page, large diaphragm muscles are raising and lowering your rib cage to help you breathe. Stop reading for a few minutes and pay attention to your ribs. Think about your diaphragm muscles as air moves in and out of your lungs. If your body needed to vomit, these same diaphragm muscles would contract fast with a lot of force, pushing the contents of your stomach up through your esophagus and out of your mouth.

You may think of puking as a bad thing: it makes your stomach hurt and smells gross. In the animal world, though, vomiting helps animals in many ways. It can scare away predators, feed family and neighbors, help with digestion, and so much more.

Wild animals are different from people and their pets. Herbivores cannot call the Poison Control Center or 911 if they eat toxic berries or leaves. Instead, they vomit. Flies and cockroaches do not have a pancreas or a liver to secrete the enzymes that help their stomachs break down their foods. Instead, they vomit and spit enzymes from their stomachs onto their food before eating. Blue jays and bears cannot go to the

grocery store for jars of baby food or cut their own food into small pieces with knives and forks to feed their young. Instead, they vomit up some partially digested food for their babies.

If you hear your friends or your family saying, "Grrrrrrooosssss," as they read through this book, please remind them that the gross and weird things we see in nature help animals compete and survive. Animal puke isn't gross: it's really pretty cool.

Have fun getting *The Scoop on Animal Puke!*

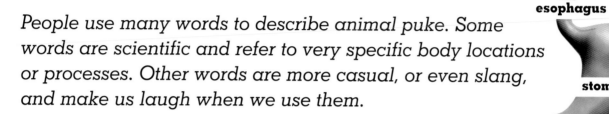

People use many words to describe animal puke. Some words are scientific and refer to very specific body locations or processes. Other words are more casual, or even slang, and make us laugh when we use them.

esophagus

stomach

intestines

SCIENTIFIC/MEDICAL WORDS AND PHRASES

ALIMENTARY CANAL: The digestive tract in vertebrate animals; begins with the mouth and ends with the anus. Many areas of the tube, such as the stomach, have adaptations that help them do their jobs better.

DIGEST (digestion): The process of breaking down consumed food into small molecules that an organism can use.

EMESIS: The forceful movement of the stomach's contents up through the mouth; vomiting.

ENZYME: A type of protein that makes reactions happen in organisms. Digestive enzymes play important roles in helping organisms break down the foods they eat into chemical energy that their bodies need to live.

ESOPHAGUS: The tube that brings food from the mouth to the stomach.

PROJECTILE VOMITING: Vomiting with great force, which often causes the vomit to move a great distance through the air. See page 19 for an example.

REGURGITATE: The vomiting of partially digested food. See pages 46 through 54 for examples in a variety of animals.

VOMITING: See Emesis.

VOMITUS: Vomit

SLANG WORDS AND PHRASES

BARFING (barf), BLOWING CHUNKS, LOSING YOUR LUNCH, PUKING (puke),

RETCHING, THROWING UP, TOSSING COOKIES, UPCHUCKING

On one *level, the science behind animal puke in most animals is simple: food goes in through the mouth, down through the esophagus and into the stomach. Foods are broken down into small molecules in the stomach, and then move into the small intestine to be absorbed into the body. The digestive systems that cause animals to puke (or not!) are usually well adapted for their specific habitats, foods, and predators. When you see differences in digestive systems, it's fun to think about how those differences work to help animals compete better.*

Fast Thinking

The vomit control center in the brain tells muscles in and around the stomach to contract, forcing food back through the esophagus, and out the mouth.

Drool Fools

Why do so many animals (including people) produce extra saliva right before they puke? Scientists aren't sure. It may be to help protect teeth enamel from stomach acid. It could also be because the Vomit Control Center in the brain is right next to the part of the brain that controls saliva production.

Now? Later? Never?

How do animals know when to vomit? Their nervous systems collect information from inside and outside their bodies, and send that information to the Vomit Control Center.

Animals vomit to protect themselves from toxins and from predators. When an animal's body recognizes a toxin in its stomach, its brain's vomit control center turns on, telling its body to puke. In fearful situations, such as when predators threaten them, animals may puke as part of their fight or flight instincts. Less food in their stomachs means less body weight and more oxygen-moving blood available for large muscles to help them escape. Animals vomit for other reasons, too, as you will see in this book.

Bugs Puke, Too?

Yes, bugs vomit, too, for many of the same reasons other animals vomit.

Puke Protection

Large predators such as lions may not need to use their fight or flight instincts very often. Vomiting can still help these large predators if they eat diseased prey animals, though.

Puke Isn't Perfect

Cockroach puke may deter small predators, such as insects, but larger predators, such as this lizard, do not mind a little puke with their cockroach dinners.

Danger Lurks

When animals vomit, the sounds they make tell hungry predators where to find them. Many animals cannot see or smell approaching predators while they are vomiting, making them even more vulnerable.

NO PUKERS HERE

Several types of animals cannot vomit, which prevents them from puking up things in their stomachs that could hurt or kill them. Horses and rabbits, for example, can regurgitate food from their esophagus, but once it gets to their stomachs, strong valves seal shut and will not open for vomit to move back up.

Biologists do not know why elephants cannot puke, but there are only a few documented case of barfing elephants.

Note to Brain: Please Talk to My Diaphragm!

Some animals, such as rats (left), guinea pigs (right), and Japanese quail, cannot throw up, usually because their diaphragm muscles and their brains do not work the same way they do in other animals. Animals that cannot vomit usually have excellent senses of taste and smell.

Fatal Mistakes

Land turtles can vomit, but marine turtles cannot. When marine turtles eat ocean trash, it stays in their stomachs if it's too big to move through their intestines. Having trash in their stomachs can change their buoyancy, which makes them unable to dive below the water's surface to feed. Why do marine turtles eat trash, you may be asking? Many biologists believe soft plastic bottles and containers look like one of the turtles' favorite foods, jellyfish.

I Need a Stomach!

Animals with incomplete digestive systems, such as jellyfish and sponges, do not have stomachs. Their food comes in through the same opening that their waste goes out.

RIGHT:
Japanese quail

PEOPLE PUKE

People vomit for many of the same reasons that other animals do: to remove toxins from our bodies, when we are very afraid, and when we have infections from disease-causing organisms such as viruses, bacteria, and parasites. The norovirus (right), for example, causes thousands of people to throw up every year. Some people also vomit from motion sickness when they go on roller coasters, or travel by planes, boats, or cars.

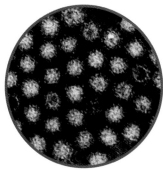

See & Smell

People often feel sick or gag when they see or smell things such as molding foods and feces. These responses may protect us by warning us not to eat things that can make us sick.

Upside Down

Some people get sick when they go on carnival rides. Other people get sick when they see or smell someone else's puke, which is called sympathy vomiting.

PUKE DEFENSE

Many sea birds defend themselves and their chicks with vomit. Because they nest on rocky cliffs, they cannot hide their nests in trees the way many other birds do, leaving them more vulnerable to predators. Their vomit doesn't just dribble out of their mouths. Instead, it moves out of their bodies with force, often flying several feet through the air. This type of vomit is called projectile vomit.

ABOVE: Albatross birds projectile vomit a fishy oil to protect themselves and their chicks from predators.

A Lot to Protect

Most northern fulmar birds (below and right) do not begin breeding until they are eight to ten years old. Females lay just one egg per year. Without their vomit defense, these birds would have gone extinct long ago. Their vomit smells like fish oil because of the fish they eat.

Easy Prey? No way!
Fish-Oil Vomit Saves the Day

PUKE DEFENSE

Vulture Vomit

Turkey vultures (right) and other types of vultures feed on dead animals called carrion. Some-times, the prey animals have been dead for just a few minutes, while other times they have been dead for days. If another animal tries to attack a feeding vulture or steal its food, the vulture vomits on them. Vulture vomit is not ordinary vomit — it contains rotting flesh, bacteria, and parasites. Like many sea birds, a vulture's stomach acid is much stronger than the acid in other animals' stomachs.

LEFT: Young Eurasian roller birds vomit on themselves when a predator threatens them. The vomit discourages predators from eating them, and parents come rushing back when they smell their offspring's vomit. The next time you need help from your parents, think about how lucky you are not to be a Eurasian roller!

Falsely Accused

Have you ever heard that camels spit when they feel threatened? Actually, camel "spit" is really a frothy vomit that is released by the camel's stomach a little at a time. People who live and work with camels say this stomach spit smells horrible. Should we take their word for it or start a scientific study?

Many kinds of insects vomit to defend themselves, including butterflies, moths, beetles, ants, termites, roaches, bees, wasps, mantids, grasshoppers, crickets, katydids, and flies. This behavior is called defensive regurgitation. The vomit usually has irritants or chemicals in it that repel predators. Insect puke is not strong enough to protect bugs from large predators, but since many insect predators are other insects or spiders that are similar in size, defensive regurgitation is worth the effort.

Scary Surprise

The sudden appearance of stinky vomit often startles predators, giving the puking insects a little extra time to escape.

Bug Barf to The Rescue

Insect-eating birds remember which insects taste bad and avoid them. Bug barf makes an impression!

TOXIC PUKE DEFENSE

Defensive regurgitation packs more power in its punch when the puke has toxins in it. The puke becomes toxic when the insects feed on plants that produce toxins to protect themselves from herbivores. Some insects, such as monarch butterflies that feed on milkweed plants, have developed immunity to the milkweed toxins through mutations passed down from one generation of butterflies to the next.

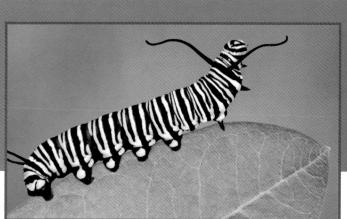

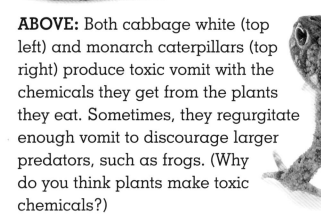

ABOVE: Both cabbage white (top left) and monarch caterpillars (top right) produce toxic vomit with the chemicals they get from the plants they eat. Sometimes, they regurgitate enough vomit to discourage larger predators, such as frogs. (Why do you think plants make toxic chemicals?)

RIGHT: Some predators, such as the mantid and the spider shown here, are not bothered by the monarch's milkweed defense.

Toxic Taunts

When a bird eats a milkweed-feeding monarch, the bird throws up. If monarch butterflies could talk, they might be taunting birds with, *"Ha, ha, made you puke!"* Viceroy mimic butterflies look a lot like monarchs, but do not taste bad or make birds puke. If viceroy mimics could talk, they might be laughing and telling birds, *"Ha, ha, faked you out."*

VICEROY MIMIC

INDIGESTIBLE PUKE

Birds of prey (owls, eagles, petrels, hawks, and other raptors) swallow their food whole. Their stomachs have two chambers, one that works like our stomach, and another, the gizzard, that crushes food into small pieces. (Remember, birds do not have teeth to chew their food.) The gizzard also works like a filter, preventing things like bones and feathers from going into the main stomach chamber. When their gizzards are full, birds must vomit up the contents of their gizzards — called a pellet — before they can eat again.

Pellet Power

The shape of a bird's gizzard determines the shape of its pellets. If you dissect a pellet in science class, you can find clues about the bird's diet: mouse skulls, songbird feathers, bat wings, and more.

Look up

The next time you're in the woods, use pellet clues to find owl habitats. Owls return home after feeding, so you can usually find a collection of pellets under their trees.

Coughing Puke

A bird can look like it is vomiting, coughing, or choking when it regurgitates a pellet from its gizzard. Pellets usually come up quickly, though, and do not damage or hurt the bird.

Birds of prey are not the only pellet pukers. Fish-eating birds regurgitate pellets with bones in them, and insect-eating birds sometimes regurgitate pellets made from exoskeletons and wings. Some fruit-eating birds regurgitate pellets made from seeds and skin.

A seagull regurgitating-- a pellet

INDIGESTIBLE PUKE

When carnivores eat parts of their prey such as bones that their bodies cannot digest, the indigestible parts usually move through the lower part of their alimentary canals, leaving their bodies as waste in their feces. Carnivores that eat prey with large or sharp parts often remove these indigestible items through their upper alimentary canals by vomiting them out.

Vomit Fossils

Biologists in Britain have found fossilized vomit from an ichthyosaur, a marine reptile from the Jurassic time period. Ichthyosaurs ate squid-like animals called belemnites. The fossilized vomit was filled with belemnite shells!

Sperm whales eat hundreds of pounds of squid every day. They vomit up the squids' sharp beaks instead of moving them out through their intestines in feces.

Hyena Hairballs

Hyenas vomit undigested pieces of bones, hooves, and fur from the mammals they eat. Sometimes, they roll in their vomit before hunting to disguise their scent from prey.

Ouch!

Seals and sea lions vomit pieces of undigested fish and bird bones.

INDIGESTIBLE PUKE

Like other carnivores, snakes, lizards, crocodiles, alligators, and other reptiles vomit the parts of their food they cannot digest. They also vomit for many of the same reasons as other animals. Many snakes, for instance, vomit their meals when they feel threatened. They cannot move fast if they have a belly full of food and a predator approaches, so vomiting helps them escape with their lives.

Scrambled or Over Easy?

High-protein eggs are a favorite food for many snakes, but the shells are hard to digest. To solve this problem, snakes use sharp points on the insides of their backbones to crack the shells as the eggs move through their bodies, and then regurgitate the shells back out. Some lizards also vomit shells.

Coolest Job Ever

How would you like to research the ways crocodiles puke? Scientists from London went to Australia to study vomiting in crocodiles. Researchers gave the crocodiles toxins to make them throw up, and then measured their blood pressure and heart activity. They also videotaped the vomiting crocs.

What did the researchers learn? Crocodiles make a lot of noise when they puke! They leap forward and snap their jaws, as if they are striking at prey, then shake their heads from side to side. Why do crocodiles shake their heads when they puke? Biologists believe their diaphragm muscles may not be strong enough to force the puke all the way out of their mouths. Alligators and gavials, close relatives of crocodiles, may vomit the same way.

BABY PUKERS

Almost everything in nature is worth careful observation. For instance, why do the frogs below have big, bulging throats? And what about the fish on the right-hand page? Are they vomiting or regurgitating? Research always rewards you with great stories!

Male Darwin's frogs from Chile and Argentina bring their fertilized eggs into their mouths and into their vocal sacs, where the eggs will grow into young frogs. When it's time for the young froglets to leave, the father regurgitates them out through his mouth. This type of parent protection is called gastric brooding.

A recent study of Darwin's frogs shows their numbers are going down and that they are found in fewer places. Biologists believe that another species of Darwin's frog in South America and two species of gastric-brooding frogs from Australia have been extinct for several decades.

Gastric-Brooding Dads

Puking Fish

Several types of fish, including the cardinal fish (left) and the jawfish (below) protect their eggs in their mouths while the embryos grow. In some species, the parents do not eat while they are mouth brooding. In other species, the parents briefly expel the eggs to eat, and then suck them back in again.

PUKE SOUP

Vomiting digestive enzymes onto your food may sound gross, but it's the only way some spiders and insects can feed. The enzymes break the foods down into smaller pieces (molecules) that are easier to digest. These same types of enzymes work in your stomach and your saliva to break down the foods you eat into small molecules that can be absorbed into your bloodstream.

Bad Reputation

Spiders use enzymes in their vomit in different ways, depending on the type of spider and the type of food they're eating. Large spiders tend to crush their prey, and then regurgitate digestive enzymes on top of it before sucking in their food as a liquid. Smaller spiders, such as the crab spider shown above, vomit digestive enzymes into the fang holes they make in their prey.

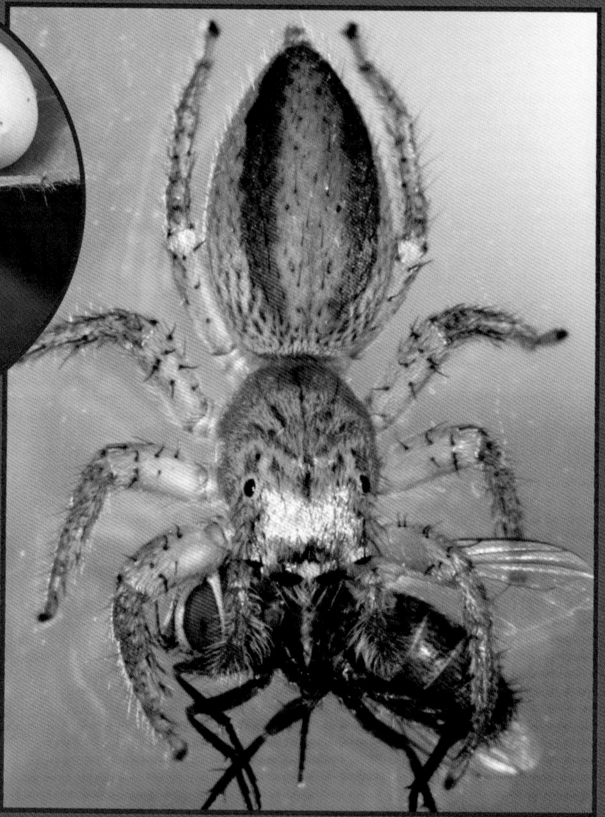

Puking for a Cause

Many people believe houseflies vomit every time they land. Actually, the flies are drooling or spitting saliva from their stomachs that contains digestive enzymes.

Like houseflies, cockroaches regurgitate digestive enzymes as they feed. They also vomit up some undigested food when they feed. The smell of the vomit and enzymes left by feeding cockroaches calls more cockroaches to the scene.

Calling All Roaches

Cockroaches also defecate (poop) while they eat. Roach vomit and poop can cause dangerous diseases in people, so try not to share your food with roaches.

PUKE DETECTIVES

Think about the ways animals protect themselves for a few minutes. Which animals crossed your mind? Snakes and their venom? Lions and their powerful jaws or sharp teeth? Now think about the ways plants defend themselves. Since their roots anchor them in the ground, plants are "sitting ducks" in some ways, unable to escape while their herbivore predators eat them. It turns out, though, that plants have some pretty amazing ways to protect themselves.

Vomit Cries for Help

Biologists have known for a while that plants can release chemicals into the air that attract the enemies of insects and spiders feeding on them. They didn't know until just recently, though, how plants do it.

When insects and spiders chew on plants, saliva and digestive juices from their stomachs send chemical messages to the plants. The plants respond by releasing

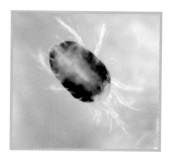

chemicals into the air that attract the biters' predators. Imagine you're a caterpillar, munching away on leaves, when in swoops one of your biggest predators, a wasp. Even if you're camouflaged or hiding under leaves, there's no hiding from a plant's chemical cues!

Caterpillar Spit Science

Biologists have done some fun experiments to find out how plants send out chemical calls for help. First, they used machines to make cuts in leaves, and then tested the chemicals the plants released. When they added some caterpillar spit to the cuts, the plants released chemicals that attracted caterpillar predators!

ABOVE and ABOVE RIGHT:
A research plant and the spit-test research caterpillar, the tobacco hornworm.

CUD PUKERS

Camels, giraffes, antelopes, cows, deer, goats, and sheep have four sections or chambers in their stomachs, and digesting the plants they eat is a long process. To start, their food spends several hours in the first stomach chamber, where bacteria help break it down. Several hours later, the animals regurgitate up their food — which is now called cud — then they chew it some more and swallow it again.

Chewing on a wad of vomited food may sound gross to us, but this extra chewing time adds more digestion enzymes to the food and helps the animals get more nutrition from the plants. Smaller plant pieces move to the third and fourth stomach chambers, while the larger ones can be coughed up again as cud.

SMALL INTESTINE
ESOPHAGUS

A View From Inside

Tough Chewing

Why does it take so much work (and four stomach chambers!) for these vegetarian animals to digest their food? The plants they eat have cell walls made from cellulose, which is a very difficult molecule to break down, or digest. Just one cellulose molecule can contain more than 10,000 glucose units in long, spiraling chains. Care to guess how many cellulose molecules are in one plant leaf?

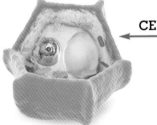

← CELL WALL

PLANT CELL

**TWISTING CELLULOSE MOLECULE
FOUND IN CELL WALLS**

CUD PUKERS

Animals with four-chambered stomachs that regurgitate chewed food are called ruminants (room-in-ants). The word ruminant comes from the Latin language, and means "chewing over again." The first and largest stomach chamber in a ruminant animal is called the rumen.

A+ Test Day

You may see a similar word, *ruminate*, on your spelling list someday. The word *ruminate* means to think about something over and over. You might use it in a sentence this way: *I ruminate about my birthday cake for 364 days every year!* Triple chocolate chip with chocolate whipped cream? Strawberry cake with vanilla pudding in between the layers? Sprinkles? Ice cream? Yum, let's ruminate about it some more . . .

More Ruminants!

TOP RIGHT: A ruminating goat
BELOW RIGHT: Bull elk
BELOW: Sheep

CUD PUKERS

Marsupials such as ground kangaroos, tree kangaroos, wallabies, and a few others also regurgitate their partially digested food. They chew cud, too, but not as often as ruminants do. Biologists believe these marsupials cough up cud to help them secrete more saliva. The plants they eat come from very dry environments and do not have much water in them. The extra saliva from coughing up their cud may help the animals get more liquid into their stomachs. Saliva also has digestive enzymes in it.

TREE KANGAROO

KANGAROO

WALLABIES

More Plant Pukers

The wombat and koala bear, both from Australia, and the proboscis monkey from Indonesia, also cough up chewed food to help them get nutrients from plants.

PROBOSCIS MONKEY

WOMBAT

Like kangaroos and wallabies, pademelons (below) chew their cud, but do not have four-chambered stomachs.

KOALA BEAR

CUD PUKERS?

Whales and dolphins have four-chambered stomachs, too, even though they do not eat hard-to-digest plants like other ruminant mammals. They inherited these four-chambered stomachs from their land-living ancestors.

When lots of food is available, whales and dolphins can fill all four stomach chambers.

Cud-Free Zone

Hippos have three-chambered stomachs, too, but they digest food the way people do, not like cud-chewing ruminants. Can you imagine a hippo coughing up a cud? Yowza, that would be one large cud!

Only Three For Me!

Camels, alpacas, and llamas have three-chambered stomachs, and are often called pseudo-ruminants (pseudo = false). The difference in their stomach structure may help these animals live in drier environments. Pseudo-ruminants do regurgitate and chew cud.

COURTSHIP PUKE

It may sound like a gross way to get a girlfriend, but males in many bird species feed females with fresh or regurgitated food. This behavior is called courtship feeding. Sometimes, courtship feeding happens when a pair first meets, but other times it happens after they have mated. Why, oh why, would birds do this? Courtship feeding proves to females that males will be able to find and share food with chicks, proving they will be good fathers.

Above and Top: Two pairs of greenfinches courtship feeding

Eggs Matter

Courtship feeding may also help females produce more or healthier eggs, or save females from hunting for food when their bodies are heavy with eggs. Males may also feed females when the females are incubating their eggs so the eggs will be safe from predators and stay the right temperatures.

ABOVE and **LEFT:** Parrots and budgies courtship feeding

Insect Courtship Puke?

In a few species, male spiders and insects feed females as part of courtship, and most of them use smaller insects as the food. In fruit flies, males vomit up a nutritious liquid food from their stomachs and feed it — one drop at a time — to females.

PUKE FEEDERS

Mammal moms feed their newborns with milk. As the babies get older and larger, they need more than milk, but it may not be safe for them to leave their burrows to hunt with their parents. Instead, some parents regurgitate food to feed their young after a hunt. In some species, only moms regurgitate food; in other species, both parents do. In species that live in packs, such as wolves and coyotes, non-relatives also regurgitate food for the young.

Good Dads

Male wolves bring regurgitated food to nursing females in their dens. Sound gross? How would you feed your family if you could not get food from your garden, a grocery store, or a restaurant?

Bear Food

Female panda, grizzly, and black bears also feed their cubs with regurgitated food. In Sri Lanka and India, female sloth bears wean their cubs with regurgitated fruit and honeycomb. Instead of placing the food in their cubs' mouths, the moms vomit on the ground. The cubs eat the vomit after it hardens, and local people call it bear's bread.

46

No Fear Here

Vampire bats live in large groups in caves and hollow trees in Central and South America. At night, they feed on blood from mammals and birds. When they return home, the bats that found food share with bats that did not find food by regurgitating blood into the hungry bat's mouth. This type of cooperation is called reciprocal altruism.

Family Food

Both jackal parents regurgitate food for their young. Sometimes, the father regurgitates food for the mom to share with the pups. Older brothers and sisters also regurgitate food for their younger siblings. In coyotes (below), both parents and other pack members regurgitate food for their young. Raccoon moms also feed their kits this way.

PUKE FEEDERS

Food Fight!

First impressions are not always trustworthy in nature. These ants may look like they're fighting, but the larger one is feeding the smaller one.

When worker ants feed on nectar, some of the food goes to their stomachs and some goes to a storage area called the crop. When these ants meet younger ants or larvae, they feed their relatives by regurgitating food from their crops.

Scam Plan

Some types of beetles can convince ants to feed them. When the beetle taps the ant with its antennae in just the right place, the ant vomits for the beetle the same way it would vomit for another ant. The next time you're playing outside and feel thirsty, maybe you should search for ants? Oh, wait, you don't have antennae . . .

Sharing Sweet Treats

One type of worker ant, called the honey ant replete, spends its days hanging upside down from the ceilings of underground nests. Their stretchy abdomens expand to more than eight times their normal size to hold the food other worker ants regurgitate into their mouths! During droughts, replete ants regurgitate honeydew and nectar from their swollen stomachs to feed their nest mates. Not all ant species have honey ant repletes.

Word of the Day

TROPHALLAXIS: When animals that live in groups (usually social insects) feed each other regurgitated food or feces.

From the Greek word *allaxis*, **meaning to exchange**

PUKE FEEDERS

Most birds feed their newborn chicks with regurgitated fish, insects, worms, or seeds. The parent bird places its beak inside the open mouth of the hatchling, and then releases the food. In species with very long beaks, the babies place their beaks inside their parents' mouths. The bright colors inside the chicks' mouths and their begging sounds signal the parents' brains to go find more food.

Messy Nest

Brown pelican parents feed their hatchlings by regurgitating fish for them on the bottom of their nest. After a week and a half, the chicks start eating from their parents' bills, the way other birds do.

Yuck? Does vomit taste bad to baby birds? No! As soon as the parent bird moves its beak out of a baby's mouth, the nestling or hatchling opens its mouth back up and begs for more!

Crop Food

Unlike the mammals on pages 46 and 47, regurgitated food in birds comes from their crop, and not from their stomachs. (See the illustration on page 53 to learn where a bird's crop is located.)

Believe it or not, mammals are not the only animals that feed their young with milk. Some birds produce milk for their hatchlings in special cells in their crops. Like mammal milk, crop milk is high in sugars, proteins, and fats, which help young animals grow. Birds that make crop milk include flamingos (left and below), penguins (top right), and pigeons (below right). In flamingos, milk is also made in glands along the digestive tract. The chicks feed on crop milk for two months.

Worth the Wait

Male emperor penguins incubate their eggs while females go on long hunts for food. If a chick hatches before its mom returns, the male feeds the newborn with crop milk. Without crop milk, the chick would die.

It Takes Two

In mammals, only females produce milk. In crop milk birds, both males and females produce milk for their young.

Check It Out

The crop is a sac at the end of a bird's esophagus used to store food. Biologists believe the crop is an adaptation that helps birds collect extra food very quickly. Getting food faster takes less energy and shortens the time birds are visible to predators. This illustration shows a bird's digestive tract in purple.

CROP

PUKE FEEDERS

Honeybees live in large social groups, and each bee has a special job. Forager bees (a type of worker bee) collect sweet nectar from flowers. The nectar is stored in the bee's crop, which is also called

its honey stomach. When the forager bee returns to the hive, she feeds the nectar in her crop to another type of worker bee, a processor bee.

Chemistry Class

Honeybee homes are called hives, and hives contain small compartments called cells. In some cells, processor bees regurgitate the nectar from their crops over and over until they fill the cell. They also regurgitate an enzyme that breaks the nectar sugar into two smaller sugars, glucose and fructose. Enzymes are special proteins that make reactions happen.

After filling a cell with nectar and enzymes, worker bees fan the cells with their wings to remove extra water. Next, worker bees cover each cell with a cap made from wax secreted by their bodies.

In some cells, the hive's queen lays a single egg that will grow into a larva and then a pupa.

Good Reasons!

During the winter, when flowers have stopped blooming, honeybees use their honey as a food source.

PUKE BUILDERS

New Construction

To build a new colony, worker bees use wax scales that form under their bodies to form the six-sided cells that will become a new hive's honeycomb. Only bees that are well fed can produce wax. Workers feed on honey from the old hive before leaving, storing extra in their crop and regurgitating it when needed.

Future queens grow in special cocoon-like cells called royal cups. Queen larvae are fed royal jelly, a high-protein food secreted from glands on worker bees' heads. Royal jelly turns off the genes that make worker bees, and the larvae that eat it grow into egg-laying queens.

Yum, Yum

People rarely think about honeybee vomit when they spread honey on muffins or sweeten their drinks with it.

PUKE BUILDERS

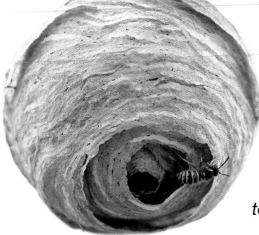

The idea of building large houses from puke sounds like it belongs in a science fiction novel. Social (group-living) wasps and termites do it all the time, though. Their homes even contain separate compartments with rooms and shapes that protect their eggs, repel rainwater, and keep the temperature just right.

Paper Play

Paper wasps, hornets, and yellow jackets make paper nests from a mixture of saliva and regurgitated wood and plant fiber. The shape and size of the nest depends on the species and where it lives. Although paper nests look thin and delicate, they are very strong.

Adult wasps, hornets, and yellow jackets regurgitate food for their newly hatched larvae. In some types of wasps, recently fed larvae can regurgitate a sugary, soup-like puke back to the adults!

Mud Puke Homes

Termites build their homes (called mounds) from a mixture of soil, saliva, feces, and regurgitated wood. This mixture is called termite mud. Inside the mounds, worker termites regurgitate food for newly hatched nymphs for about two weeks.

Termite mounds affect the environment in many ways. In Africa, animals such as the yellow mongoose, the topi antelope, and the cheetah use mounds to search for faraway predators and/or prey. In Australia, reptiles, birds, and small marsupials use termite mounds as nests.

Termite mounds benefit plants because the feces from millions of termites adds nutrients to the soil.

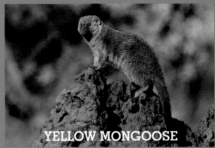
YELLOW MONGOOSE

TOPI ANTELOPE

CHEETAH

PARASITE PUKE

Ticks, fleas, flies, and mosquitoes cause disease in humans and our pets. Females need blood meals to produce eggs, which is why they bite. During biting and blood feeding, females can transfer parasites, bacteria, and viruses from their stomachs and saliva. These types of animals are called disease vectors. Some parasite diseases in birds are passed from one bird to another when birds regurgitate food for their young or for mates.

Worse Than an Itch or a Pinch . . .

Ticks can pass many types of disease-causing parasites that make both pets and people very ill. Fleas pass tapeworms to their hosts when they regurgitate parts of their blood meals. Fleas can also pass disease-causing bacteria and viruses, and were responsible for thousands of human deaths during the bubonic and Italian plagues. Female horse flies and deer flies also transfer diseases to animals when they bite.

Vector Buzz

Female mosquitoes cause many types of diseases around the world. In Africa, malaria causes more than 300,000 deaths every year, and thousands more people live with malaria-related sicknesses. **Above right:** Note the red, blood-filled abdomen of a biting female mosquito. **Above left:** A *Plasmodium* parasite from a human blood sample. This parasite causes malaria.

Break the Zombie Cycles: Stop Eating Puke

Vomit plays an important role in the life cycle of a parasite called the lancet fluke. Adult parasites live in plant-eating mammals. The parasites produce millions of eggs, which exit their mammal hosts' bodies in feces (poop). When snails eat the feces, the parasite eggs move into their bodies. The eggs hatch into small larvae inside the snails, and the snails' stomachs coat the young larvae with mucus. Later, they vomit up the mucus-covered larvae.

Still reading? Wondering whether this life cycle ever ends?

Next, ants eat the mucus vomit, and the larvae grow larger inside the ants. Ants with lancet flukes inside them behave in strange ways, which is why they are called zombie ants. Instead of staying in their safe nests, zombie ants climb to leaves and hang on with their jaws. When plant-eating mammals feast on the leaves, they eat infected ants with their plants. Once the flukes are back inside the stomach of a mammal host, the larvae grow into adults and release millions of eggs, beginning the cycle again. There are many other types of zombie animals. Research some of them!

HOUSEKEEPING PUKE

Just like the animals on pages 26 through 29, the animals here eat things they cannot digest. Instead of just puking up those things, though, these animals vomit out their entire stomachs and then bring them back inside their bodies. This process is called stomach rinsing, stomach eversion, or gastric eversion.

Why, Oh Why?

Biologists who study rays believe they may rinse their stomachs to clean out old mucus, dead cells, and indigestible pieces of food.

Pebble Trouble

Land turtles often vomit out their stomachs when trying to empty small rocks from their stomachs. The stones were probably mistaken for food.

60

Why Can't We Do It?

Frogs eject their stomachs to quickly remove bad foods, and have even been seen wiping off their stomachs with their front legs. Do not let this image cross your mind the next time you puke, though. The animals shown here can vomit up their stomachs because their esophagus tubes are very wide and elastic, which allows them to swallow large food items. A human esophagus tube is too narrow and not stretchy enough for our stomachs to move through.

Sharks vomit their stomachs to remove things such as undigested turtle shells or human trash.

ROCK PUKERS

Some birds eat small rocks and stones on purpose. The rocks and stones go to their gizzards, the grinding stomach chamber in birds. Rocks and stones may help gizzard muscles work better by giving the muscles something sharp to push against. After a while, the rocks and stones get smaller and smoother, so the birds puke them up and swallow new, sharper ones to replace them.

Rock Eaters

Ground birds such as ostriches (left), emus (below left), and chickens (below right) eat stones. The stones help the birds break apart the bones in prey foods such as small lizards.

Paleontologists have also found stones in the fossilized stomachs of aquatic animals such as penguins, seals, alligators, crocodiles, and dinosaurs.

Word of the Day

GASTROLITH: From the Greek words *gastro* and *lith*, which translates to stomach stones.

PUKING STOMACHS

Some sea stars (also called starfish) feed by pushing their outer stomach section through their mouths, which are on the under sides of their bodies. Their stomachs release digestive enzymes to break down their food, then small hairs push the food pieces into their mouths. Sea stars can even push their stomachs into a clam or mussel shell after their feet pry it open!

Eating on the Run

Sea stars have thousands of tiny tube feet on the under sides of their bodies, letting them eat and walk at the same time.

Ecosystem Nightmare

The crown-of-thorns star-fish (above) eats so much coral on Australia's Great Barrier reefs that it is destroying the ecosystem. This starfish has venom-filled spines, so it has few predators.

Humans do not eat vomit, but many organisms will eat as much animal puke as they can find. Small animals such as snails, spiders, and insects often eat puke, and so do bacteria and fungi. In nature, where there are many hungry organisms and not enough food to go around, vomit is a welcome food source.

No Waste Here

Fungi get food energy in a much different way than people do. If we were eating a blueberry cheesecake, we would take small bites, chew it up in our mouths, break it down in small pieces in our stomachs, absorb the useful nutrients in our small intestines, and then move the leftover waste out of our bodies as feces. Wow, that's a lot of work! A fungus takes in only the sugars, fats, and proteins that it can use, and leaves the waste behind. If a pile of puke is nearby, a fungus will grow toward it.

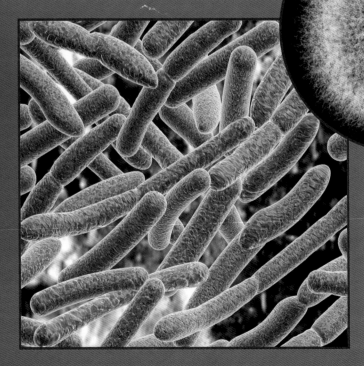

1 Today, 5 Trillion Tomorrow

Bacteria reproduce very quickly with binary fission when food is available. Just one bacterium near a pile of puke right this minute can multiply into more than five trillion bacteria by tomorrow.

WILD & WACKY

Invasive or alien species can cause a lot of damage to ecosystems. One type of sea squirt, called rock vomit, secretes toxins that damage fish and other marine animals. In parts of Alaska, rock vomit sea squirts have attached to the bottoms of ships, piers, rocks, and shells, which prevents fish from getting to their food.

No Trouble Here

Most sea squirts live their lives attached to rocks and other underwater surfaces, often as part of coral reef environments. Sea squirts are also called tunicates.

WILD & WACKY

Can houseflies paint? Look at the paintings below and ask yourself that question again. Artist John Knuth collaborates with more than 50,000 flies to make each of his paintings! John leaves the flies alone in a room with prepared canvases and bowls of water and sugar mixtures tinted with paint. When the flies land on the canvas, they regurgitate the colored sugar water onto the canvas!

RIGHT AND BELOW:
Fly paintings by artist John Knuth

Bat Spat!

Fruit bats often bring the fruit they find during foraging flights back to their roosts. As they eat, they press hard-to-digest fruit parts against the roofs of their mouths. After they swallow the juice and softer parts of the fruit, the material on the roofs of their mouths is "spat" out.

LETTER PLAY: If you add the letter *l* in the middle of the word *spat*, you get *splat*, which is used to describe the material that comes out of the other end of a fruit bat's alimentary canal!

PUKE INTERVIEW

Let's face it: Some jobs involve more puke than others. A chemical engineer may never interact with vomit at work, while veterinarians like Dr. Beth Snyder work with vomit every day. Here, Dr. Snyder answers some Puke Interview questions.

Can you tell what's wrong with an animal from its puke?

The description can be helpful and in specific cases can be diagnostic. For example, vomit that looks like coffee grounds is usually caused by a stomach ulcer. Bile-stained (yellow) vomit can be seen when a dog is nauseated. If a pet throws up a bone or a toy, then it's a good chance that was causing them to feel sick.

Can vomiting save an animal's life?

Yes. In cases where your pet has eaten a poisonous substance, then in most cases inducing vomiting within 30 minutes is very important. Some poisons do not have an antidote and vomiting is the number one thing to do. Certain plants will cause pets to throw up such as poinsettia.

What should I do if my pet is vomiting?

First, take away your pet's food and water. Continuing to offer food or water can do more harm than good. When the stomach is irritated, continuing to eat or drink doesn't give the stomach time to recover. Chronic vomiting for 24 hours will cause serious dehydration, while vomiting for a short time will not.

Do people do a good job of describing their pet's puke?

More and more, clients are using their cell phones to take pictures of their pets' vomit, which they show me in the exam room. Before cell phones, they would bring pet puke to me in plastic sandwich bags. One client even brought in the whole sofa cushion for me to see! (It turned out to be urine on the cushion, not vomit. I could tell by the smell.) When we look at vomit, we are looking for food (digested or undigested?) and foreign objects (rocks, socks, bones, etc.). It is also important to find out how often the pet is vomiting, what time of day, and how much it's vomiting.

PUKE INTERVIEW

When you are about to puke, you may not care much about what is happening in your body and why. Human puke can be just as interesting as animal puke, though. Here, Dr. Don Teater answers some human Puke Interview questions from curious kids.

Is there a good type of puke?

Yes. There are some kinds of poisons that will make you vomit them back out of your stomach before they cause any more harm to your body.

Why do we have a gag reflex?

We have a gag reflex to prevent the puke from going into our lungs. When you gag, it is actually the top of your windpipe closing off. For this to work right, it has to close up before you puke. Sometimes your brain thinks you are about to puke so it will make you gag even if you don't end up puking.

If someone has a stomach virus, is his or her puke contagious? Can you get sick from cleaning it up?

Yes, it is contagious and you can easily get sick from cleaning it up. You should wear rubber gloves if possible. Also, whether you wear gloves or not, you should wash your hands very well after cleaning up puke.

PUKE INTERVIEW

Why is puke different every time?

It depends on what you have eaten recently and how long it has been since you have eaten.

Is there a way you can stop yourself from vomiting?

There are some medicines that will help but there is nothing that you can do yourself.

Does puke still gross you out?

Yes. I think it is really gross!

Why does puke come up so fast?

Your stomach is a muscle that is very strong.

Why do you feel so weird when you're about to puke?

There are certain nerves that go to your stomach to make you puke. There are very similar nerves that go to other parts of your body and often these are all "turned on" at the same time. These other nerves will make your eyes water, your nose run, and your mouth water right before puking.

Now that you know a little about animal stomachs and puke, keep learning! All animals, regardless of how complex they are or where they live, need ways to digest their food, avoid predators, and protect their offspring. These two pages will give you some ideas to start your own research. Keep looking until you find good information, then share it with your friends.

Cruise The Web

Research the ways octopuses use ink to defend themselves. How do they make the ink? Where do they store it? Are they vomiting ink?

Velvet Worm Vomit

Ask your favorite librarian to help you find a video of a velvet worm that is feeding. Want a preview? The worms vomit up a sticky, gooey substance filled with digestive enzymes. The enzymes start breaking down the food before the worms eat it! What other animals eat this way?

Training Birds with Vomit

Use the search terms "vomit eggs" and "training birds" to look up the work biologists are doing to save the marbled murrelet (left), an endangered bird found on the coast of California.

Peeeww . . .

Read about plants such as the gingko tree that smell like puke. Is this an adaptation that helps them avoid predators or attract pollinators? Look it up!

Frogs Vomiting Beetles? Really?

Some species of beetles wait for frogs to try to eat them, then jump onto the frog's neck or abdomen and suck fluids from the frog's body. If a frog eats a beetle, the frog gets sick and vomits the beetle up again. The beetle then crawls out of the vomit and attaches to the frog's skin to feed.

People Vomiting Frogs? Really?

With a little research, you can find many stories of people vomiting up frogs and other amphibians in Europe during the 1700s through the early 1900s. Back then, doctors did not know enough body chemistry to realize that amphibians would die in our stomach acid. In the 1800s, a famous frog-puking woman admitted that she had been tricking people by hiding frogs in her dress pockets until just the moment she vomited.

GLOSSARY

BACTERIA: Single-celled organisms that do not have membranes around specialized areas in their cells.

CARNIVORE: An animal or plant that eats animals. Examples include tigers, wolves, starfish, seals, sharks, crocodiles, and Venus flytraps.

CHEMICALS: Molecules made from atoms that interact in organisms and the environment. Some chemicals help animals; others hurt them.

DIGESTIVE ENZYMES: Specialized enzymes produced by organisms to help break down their foods into smaller, usable molecules. Some digestive enzymes work well on fats, while others work well on proteins or carbohydrates.

DIGESTIVE SYSTEM: The parts of an animal's body responsible for breaking down food into small, usable parts and for getting rid of unusable parts as waste. In vertebrates, the digestive system starts with the mouth and ends with the anus.

HABITAT: The home for an organism or a group of organisms.

HERBIVORE: An animal that eats plants. Examples include rabbits and zebras.

PREDATOR: An animal searching for organisms to eat.

SALIVA: A liquid secreted into the mouth by several large glands. Saliva contains water to help moisten food, mucus to soften food so it doesn't hurt the esophagus on the way to the stomach, and some digestive enzymes.

UNDIGESTIBLE: Material that an organism's body cannot break down into usable pieces. Undigestible materials leave a vertebrate animal's digestive system through vomit or feces.

RESEARCH & READING

About the Research for This Book . . .

A Note from the Author: The research in this book came from many places. I learned a lot of basic information about animals and digestive systems when I was a student, and laster as a teacher. Most of the details in this book came from journal articles where scientists report their research results. Veterinarian textbooks and some websites were also used as sources. The names of the scientists, authors, organizations, and websites are listed on page 78.

Learning more about the future readers of this book — kids! — was another important part of the research process. To discover more about what kids like about animal puke and what types of questions they have, I worked with students, teachers, and the librarian at Hall Fletcher Elementary School in Asheville, North Carolina. Students read early drafts of the book and provided helpful feedback. They also provided the interview questions for the doctor interview on pages 70 and 71. Thank you, Hall Fletcher students and librarian Beverly McBrayer!

3rd GRADE

Ms. Virginia Duquet, teacher: Akiya, Alana, Alexis, Brooklyn, Ciera, David, Diego, Esme, Evan, Gabriel, Jackie, Jonah, Kaliyah, Michon, Saril, Tyshauna, and Zyon

Mr. Brian Randall, teacher: Bryan, Destiny, Elvin, Jason, Jesus, Jorge, Jose, Kejuan, Liam, Melani, Naomi, Rashel, Sarijah, Trumaine, and Ximena

Ms. Meg Sanford, teacher: Anna, Ariel, Asher, Christopher, Dekorian, Elle, Jack, James, JeNaya, Jenesea, Julian, Kenneth, Mahayla, Micaiah, Miles, Nevaeh, and Paige

4th GRADE

Ms. Sarah Gillespie, teacher: Alison, Angel, Anthony, Antoneea, Benjamin, Bryson, Devin, Dimaiah, Elijah, Floyd, Itzel, Janiyiah, Julian, Liam, Milique, Nathaniel, Nikayia, Nolan, Rachel, Silas, Starkeisia, and Zaden

Ms. Katie McIntosh, teacher: Adam, Aiden, Alex, Amaria, Dakota, Davion, Deshawn, Elijah, Gavin, Janita, Kaleb, Kaven, Liam, Makayla, Marek, Mariq, Mark, Marqua, Melina, Michaiah, Nancy, Raven, and Sir

5th GRADE

Ms. Michele Corral, teacher: Asiya, Christopher, Delamonte, Isaiah, Jackson, Jada, Jaquese, Kaleb, Kamari, Keller, Kenyon, Lamarius, Leslie, Samuel, Savannah, Sidney, Synia, Tanyjae, and Willa

Mr. Tomas Seijo, teacher: Alexus, Anala, Cole, Daisy, Daquavion, Gabriel, Geonessy, George, Jack, Jade, Jaylin, Jaymes, Malyssa, Otus, Tira, Tony, Rodjahnneieigh, and Zephram

Ms. Rebecca Shaw-Cooke teacher: Alexis, Amani, Aniyah, Asia, August, Chyna, Daveyon, Ethan, Evangeline, Fiona, Jaliyah, Javis, Jerome, Omar, Rebekah, Rodney, Stephanie, Tristan, Zion, and Zora

Read More . . .

The Dynamic Digestive System written by John Burstein; Crabtree Publishing (2009).

A Tour of Your Digestive System written by Molly Kolpin and illustrated by Chris B. Jones; Capstone Press (2012).

Gross Things about Your Body written by John M. Shea; Gareth Stevens (2012).

SUBJECT INDEX

Acid, stomach, 11, 20
Africa, 56, 59
Alimentary canal, 10, 27, 68
Argentina, 30
Australia, 29, 30, 41, 56, 63

Bacteria, 16
Bubbling, 76

California, 73
Carnivores, 26, 28, 35, 74
Carrion, 20
Chemicals, 21, 22, 35, 74
Chile, 30
Courtship feeding, 44, 45
Crop milk, 52, 53
Crops, 47, 51–54
Cud, 36–43

Defecate, 33
Defense, 18–23, 34, 72
Defensive regurgitation, 21, 22
Diaphragm, 8, 11, 29
Digest(ing), 28, 36
Digestive system, 11, 74

Eggs, 28, 30, 31, 45, 53, 56, 58, 59
Emesis, 10
Enzymes, 8, 32, 33, 36, 40,
    54, 63, 72, 74
Esophagus, 8, 10, 11, 14, 53, 61

Feces, 16, 49, 56, 59
Fight or flight, 12
Feces, 16, 49, 56, 59
Fossils, 26

Gag reflex, 16
Gastric brooding, 30
Gastric eversion, 60
Gastrolith, 62
Gizzards, 24, 25, 62

Habitat, 74
Herbivores, 8, 22, 34, 35, 72, 74
Herbivory, 35

Incomplete digestive systems, 15
India, 46
Indigestible, 24–29, 74
Indonesia, 41

Intestines, 10, 11
London, 29

Malaria, 59
Molecules, 11, 32
Motion sickness, 17
Mouth brooding, 31

Parasites, 16, 58, 59
Pellets, 24, 25
Plants, 22, 23, 34–42, 56, 59, 69,
    73, 74
Predators, 8, 11–13, 18, 20–22,
    28, 34, 35, 45, 53, 56, 63, 72–74
Projectile vomit, 18
Protection, 11–13, 16, 18, 21,
    22, 30, 31, 35, 56. 72
Pseudo-ruminants, 43

Regurgitate, 10, 14, 22, 25, 26,
    30–33, 36, 38, 40, 43, 44, 46, 47,
    49–51, 54–56, 58, 67
Regurgitation feeding, 44–54,
Rumen, 36
Ruminants, 32–40, 42, 43

Saliva, 11, 32, 35, 40, 56, 74
Small intestines, 65
South America, 30
Sri Lanka, 46
Stomachs, 8, 10, 11, 15, 20, 24,
    36–43, 51, 54, 60–63, 65
        2-chambered, 24, 62, 63
        3-chambered, 43
        4-chambered, 36–38, 41, 42
        Honey, 54
Stomach eversion, 60
Stomach rinsing, 60
Sympathy vomiting, 17

Toxins, 12, 16, 22, 23, 29, 66
Trophallaxis, 49

Viruses, 16
Vomit, 8–30, 32–34, 36, 45, 46,
    49, 51, 55, 59–61, 64, 66, 68–73
Vomit control center, 11
Vomiting, unable to, 14, 15

What is the liquid drop outside of this fly's mouth? Vomit, of course! Flies regurgitate the extra food they store in their crops to help them dry out the water in their stored food. Some flies vomit up the droplets again and again, while other flies keep them outside of their bodies. This process is called bubbling, although the droplets are not true bubbles.

ORGANISM INDEX

BACTERIA
Bacteria, 16, 58, 64, 65, 74

VIRUSES
Fungi, 64, 65
Mold, 16

FUNGI
Norovirus, 16, 58

ANIMALS: BIRDS
Albatrosses, 18, 51
Blue jays, 8
Budgies, 44
Chickens, 12, 62
Curlew, longbilled, 11
Eagles, 24
Emus, 62
Flamingos, 52
Fulmars, 18, 19
Greenfinches, 44
Hawks, 24
Kestrel, common, 3, 25
Monarch, black-naped, 51
Murrelets, marbled 73
Oriole, Northern, 23
Ostriches, 62
Owls, burrowing, snowy, 24, 75
Parrots 44
Pelicans, 50
Penguins, 53, 62
Petrels, 24
Pigeons, 53
Quail, Japanese, 14, 79
Rollers, Eurasian, 20
Seagulls, 25
Swans, 9
Vultures, turkey, 20

ANIMALS: FISH
Cardinal fish, 31
Jawfish, 31
Rays, 60
Sharks, 61

**ANIMALS:
INSECTS & SPIDERS**
Ants, 20, 48, 49

Bees, 20, 54, 55
Beetles, 20, 49, 73
Butterflies, viceroy, cabbage
 white, 20, 32, 34, 35
Cockroaches, 13, 20, 33
Crickets, 20
Fleas, 58
Flies, deer, fruit, house, 8, 20,
 33, 45, 58, 67, 76
Grasshoppers, 20
Hornets, 56
Katydids, 20
Mantids, 20, 22
Mosquitoes, 58, 59
Moths, 20
Spiders, crab, 22, 32
Stick insects, 12
Termites, 20, 56, 57
Ticks, 58
Wasps, 20, 35, 56, 57
Yellow jackets, 56

ANIMALS: MAMMALS
Antelopes, 36, 56, 57
Bats, vampire and fruit, 47, 68
Bears, black grizzly, sloth, 8, 46
Camels, 20, 36
Cats, 2
Cheetahs, 56, 57
Cows, 36, 50
Coyotes, 46, 47
Deer, 36
Dogs, 3, 58, 69, 80
Dolphins, 42
Elephants, 14
Elk, 37
Giraffes, 36
Goats, 36, 37
Guinea pigs, 15
Hippos, 43
Horses, 14
Hyenas, 27
Jackals, 47
Kangaroos, 40
Koala, 41
Leopards, 11
Lions, 13, 34
Mice, 14

Mongooses, 56, 57
Monkeys, proboscis, 41
Pademelons, 41
Pandas, 46
Rabbits, 14, 15
Raccoons, 47
Rats, 14
Sea lions, 27
Seals, 27, 62
Sheep, 36, 37
Skunks, 12
Sugar glider, 78
Wallabies, 40
Whales, 26, 42
Wolves, 46
Wombats, 41
Yak, 36

**ANIMALS:
REPTILES & AMPHIBIANS**
Alligators, 28, 29, 62
Crocodiles, 28, 29, 62
Dinosaurs, 62
Frogs, Darwin's, lemur leaf,
 22, 30, 61, 73
Gavials, 29
Ichthyosaurs, 26
Lizards, 13, 28
Snakes, 28, 34
Turtles, 15, 60

**ANIMALS:
MISC. INVERTEBRATES**
Belemnites, 26
Clams, 63
Fluke, lancet, 59
Jellyfish, 15
Mite, spider, 34
Mussels, 63
Octopuses, 72
Plasmodia, 59
Sea stars, 63
Snails, 64, 65
Sponges, 15
Squid, 26
Tunicates, rock vomit, 66
Velvet worms, 72

ACKNOWLEDGMENTS

Information from the following individuals, places, and organizations contributed greatly to this book:

David Adam, Alaska Fisheries Science Center, P. L. R. Andrews, Paul Andrews, Arizona State University Ask a Biologist, Australian Termite Research Center, L. R. Axelsson, Henry Bernard, Idir Bitama, R. Bowen, British Trust for Ornithology, D. B. Casteel (Bureau of Entomology, Washington, D.C.), Centers for Disease Control and Prevention, Marcus Clauss, Ben Collen, Colorado State University, Andrew A. Cunningham, Department of Environment and Primary Industries/Victoria State Government/Australia, Katharina Dittmarb, David S. Dobkin, Peter Doyle, Earthwatch, Elizabeth Ehrhardt, Paul R. Ehrlich, Thomas Eisner, Martina Eleveld, Brock M. Fenton, FGCU Animal Behavior Research Group, S. Foret, C. Franklin, Helena Goscilo, Jacqualine Bonnie Grant, David Grémillet, Aaron T. Haselton, Seigo Higashi, Catherine Hill, Bert Hoelldobler, J. D. Holbrook, D.W. Holmgren, Iowa State University, Shea Jones, Christopher Kemp, Amanda Kreuder, R. Kucharski, Roger Lederer, John MacDonald, Yvon le Maho, J. Maleszka, R. Maleszka, Tom Marshall, Marsupial Society of Australia, Michiyuki Matsuda, Joanne Mattern, Mid Atlantic Apiculture & Extension Consortium, Brett Mommer, Tadahiro Murai1, Robert Nordsieck, North Carolina State University, One Amphibia Web, Deseada Parejo, Philippe Parolaa, Petre Petrov, Cliff Pickover, Aurélien Prudor, Purdue University Medical Entomology, Didier Raoult, J. Marcus Rowcliffe, Andrés Valenzuela-Sánchez, San Diego Zoo, G. J. Sanger, Linda Shaw, Matt Shipman, James Kenny Sieswerda, David W. Sims, S. Sims, Scott R. Smedley, Elizabeth A. Zimmerman Smith, Claudio Soto-Azat, Sri Lanka National Park, John G. Stoffolano, Corwin Sullivan, Texas A&M AgriLife Extension, Kathy Townsend, Augustine Tuuga, University of California Museum of Paleontology, University of Utah Genetic Learning Center, U.S. National Park Service, U.S. Virgin Islands Department of Planning and Natural Resources, Utah State University Cooperative Extension, Alberto Veloso, Guy Webster, Matt Wedel, Henri Weimerskirch, Bernard Werber, Darryl Wheye, Whitaker Center for Science and Education, Michael F. Whiting, Alex Wild, Jason Wood, Tomomi Yamada, and J. Z Young.

http://www.askabiologist.org.uk/
http://entoweb.okstate.edu/ddd/insects/termites
http://www.fcps.edu/islandcreekes/ecology/red_fox
http://www.mapoflife.org/topics/topic_573_Foregut-fermentation-in-mammals
http://www.nhptv.org/natureworks/brownpelican
http://www.outtoafrica.nl/animals/engjackal
http://www.psu.edu/dept/nkbiology/naturetrail/speciespages/coyote
http://www.stanford.edu/group/stanfordbirds/text/essays/Bird_Milkl
http://www.wolfhowl.org/behavior

Sugar gliders are possums from Australia and Tasmania. Unlike the marsupials on pages 40 and 41, they do not chew their cud. In the wild, they eat insects, nectar, and pollen. People who have sugar gliders for pets say gliders are messy eaters, often spitting chewed-up pieces of food all over the place.

Gratitude is extended to the following photographers, photographic sources, and illustrators for their visual creativity: Accord, ACEgan, Africa Studio, Lehrer, Brandon Alms, Alslutsky, Ambient Ideas, Protasov An, Andre Anita, ArchMan, Auremar, Claudio Soto-Azat, Norman Bateman, Ronald van der Beek, Belizar, Bertl123, John David Bigl, Bigstock Photo, BMJ, Willyam Bradberry, Papa Bravo, Javier Brosch, Vittorio Bruno, Andrew Burgess, Steve Byland, Catcher of Light, Tony Campbell, Centers for Disease Control and Prevention, Barnaby Chambers, Howard B. Cheek, Willee Cole, Colwell Photography, Coprid, Cotton Photo, Cynoclub, Ethan Daniels, Gerald A. DeBoer, Designua, Sukharevskyy Dmytro, Dobermaraner, Dennis Donohue, Jerry Dupree, Den Durda, E-I-E-I-O Fotos, Julius Elias, Eveleen, ExOrzist, Feather Collector, Andy Featherston, S. Ferdon, Viacheslav V. Fedorov, Susan Flashman, Four Oaks, Fritz16, Elena Gaak, Gentoo Multimedia Limited, Fred Goldstein, Jorge R. Gonzalez, Arto Hakola, Mark Higgins, Frank Hildebrand, Nataliya Hora, Lorraine Hudgins, Vitalii Hulai, Greg Hume/Creative Commons, Aleksandr Hunta, Idreamphoto, Iladm, Ingret, IPK Photography, IrinK, Eric Isselee, Istock Photo, Jumnong, Anan Kaewkhammul, Cathy Keifer, Kichigin, KOO, Vasiliy Koval, Krasowit, Krosbona, D. Kucharski, K Kucharska, Ivan Kuzmin, Henrik Larsson, Brian Lasenby, David Lech, Annelies Leeuw, Lightspring, Lizard, LNatalieJean, Michael Lynch, Madlen, Cosmin Manci, Ali Mufti, Steve Mann, Gerald Marella, Marigo20, Marques, Matteo Photos, McCarthy's PhotoWorks, Lauren Medford, Molekuulbe, Mopic, Ali Mufti, Nagel Photography, David Nagy, National Oceanic and Atmospheric Administration, NCBateman1, NCG, Northsweden, Sari O'Neal, Non15, Fedorov Oleksiy, Pacific Northwest Photo, Papik, Paulista, PathDoc, Andrey Pavlov, Photo Fun, Photomatz, Picture Partners, Plavevski, Patrycja Polechonska, Mike Price, Prill, Oded Ben-Raphael, Morley Read, Peter Reijners, Armin Rose, Michael Rosskothen, S. Rowan, Robert S., C. Salisbury, Sarah2, Menno Schaefer, Marcl Schauer, Peter Schwarz, SeeYou, Arnette Shaff, Sherjaca, Shutterstock, Kevin Sibley, John Lindsay-Smith, David Steele, Debbie Steinhausser, Tae208, Taviphoto, Jose Alberto Tejo, Decha Thapanya, Tania Thomson, Irina Tischenko, Mogens Trolle, Sergey Uryadnikov, Vishnevskiy Vasily, Chuck Wagner, Sphinx Wang, Wasanajai, Keith Wheatley, Michiel de Wit, and Xpixel.

How do Japanese quail hatchlings eat if their parents cannot regurgitate food for them? Maybe the hatchlings do not need to eat? Maybe the hatchlings catch flying and jumping insects that land in their mouths? Maybe the parents convince other animals to feed their young? After you have thought about it for a while, put your research skills to work and find out!

The End!